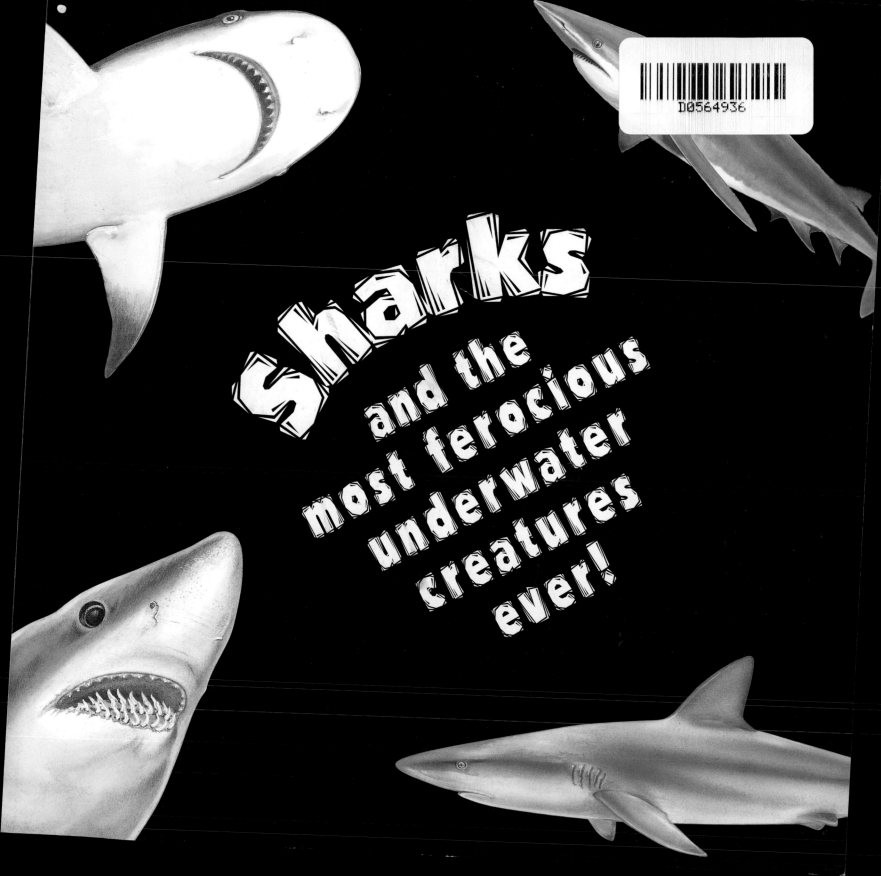

Sharks

and the most ferocious underwater creatures ever!

Authors: Valerie Davies and Elise See Tai   Consultant: Valerie Davies

Created by Pinwheel, A Division of Alligator Books Ltd
Gadd House, Arcadia Avenue, London N3 2JU, UK

Copyright © Alligator Books Ltd

This edition produced in 2008 for Scholastic Inc. 557 Broadway, New York, NY 10012

ISBN-10: 1-861-99195-9
ISBN-13: 978-1-86199-195-9

Printed in Malaysia

Contents

Ratfish

This fish is a relative of the ray and shark. It has a poisonous, needle-sharp spine, which can deliver a painful wound.

Sandbar shark

This shark is often found at the sandy bottoms of shallow waters where it feeds on small fish.

The Sandbar's triangular-shaped dorsal fin makes it easily recognizable. —

WHAT IS A SHARK?

To many people, sharks are hunting machines, packed with razor-sharp teeth. But, sharks and their relatives, rays, are fish, though they differ in several ways from other fish. The skeleton is made of cartilage, instead of bone, which is lighter and more flexible. The gill slits are not covered, as in other fish. Most sharks also have torpedo-shaped bodies to swim at speed.

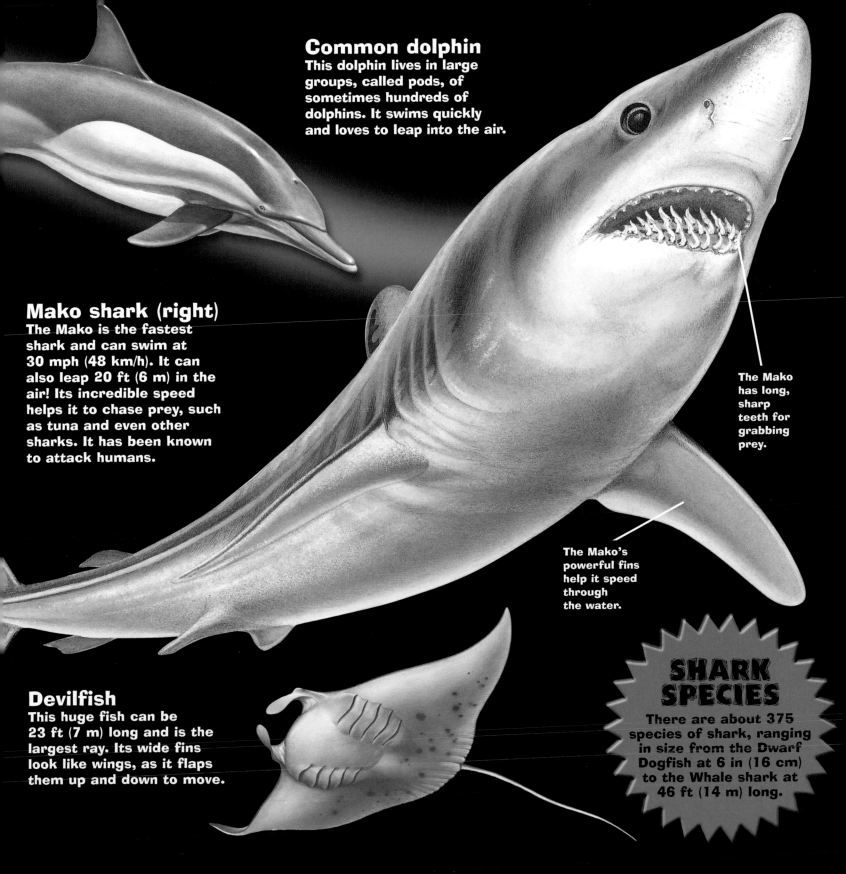

Common dolphin
This dolphin lives in large groups, called pods, of sometimes hundreds of dolphins. It swims quickly and loves to leap into the air.

Mako shark (right)
The Mako is the fastest shark and can swim at 30 mph (48 km/h). It can also leap 20 ft (6 m) in the air! Its incredible speed helps it to chase prey, such as tuna and even other sharks. It has been known to attack humans.

The Mako has long, sharp teeth for grabbing prey.

The Mako's powerful fins help it speed through the water.

Devilfish
This huge fish can be 23 ft (7 m) long and is the largest ray. Its wide fins look like wings, as it flaps them up and down to move.

SHARK SPECIES
There are about 375 species of shark, ranging in size from the Dwarf Dogfish at 6 in (16 cm) to the Whale shark at 46 ft (14 m) long.

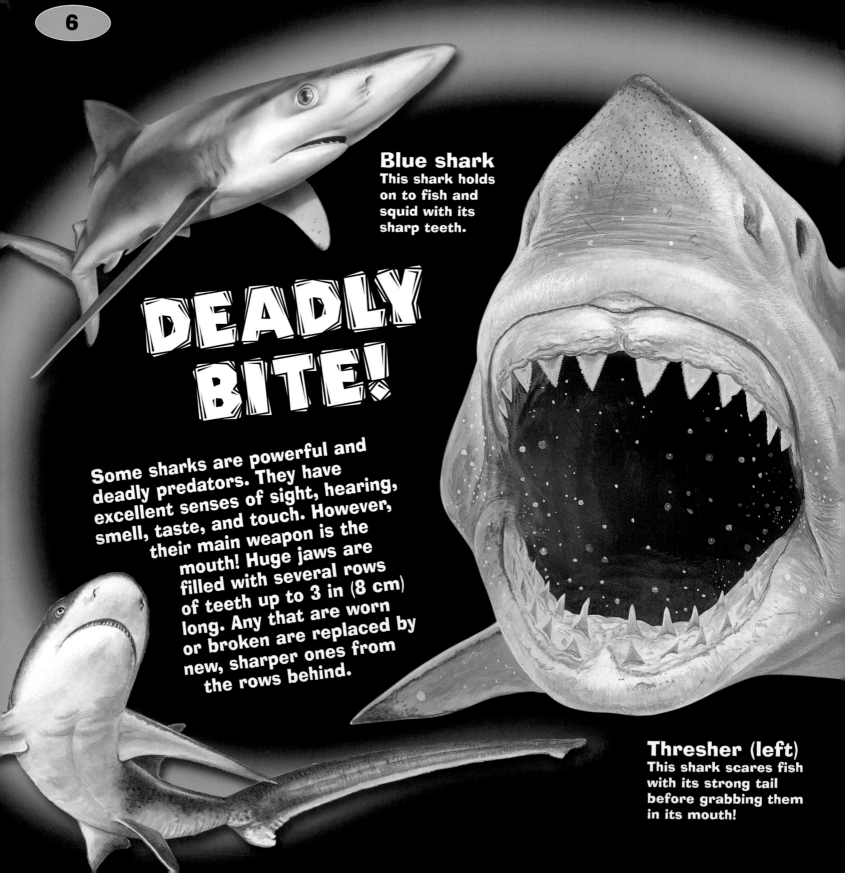

Blue shark
This shark holds on to fish and squid with its sharp teeth.

DEADLY BITE!

Some sharks are powerful and deadly predators. They have excellent senses of sight, hearing, smell, taste, and touch. However, their main weapon is the mouth! Huge jaws are filled with several rows of teeth up to 3 in (8 cm) long. Any that are worn or broken are replaced by new, sharper ones from the rows behind.

Thresher (left)
This shark scares fish with its strong tail before grabbing them in its mouth!

Tiger shark
This shark has a huge appetite and will prey on almost anything, including seals and other sharks, taking huge chunks with its sharp teeth.

Hammerhead
This shark has a unique T-shaped head, with an eye at both ends. This gives it a wide view, helping it to find prey. It uses its triangular-shaped teeth to tear off chunks of meat.

Great White shark
The Great White is one of the most feared predators in the ocean. It can have up to 3,000 sharp, jagged teeth, but it doesn't chew its food. It bites huge chunks out of its prey and swallows them whole! This hunter has been known to attack humans.

The Great White's torpedo-shaped body and powerful tail help it to reach speeds of 30 mph (48 km/h).

DID YOU KNOW?
Some Hammerheads use their heads to butt and pin down prey. They then spin round and bite pieces out of their victims!

The Great White has a powerful body with large pectoral fins.

FIERCE HUNTER!
The Great White can detect prey up to 1 mile (1.6 km) away, detect blood in water up to ½ mile (0.8 km) away, and can see prey up to 25 ft (7.6 m) away in dark water.

DEDICATED HUNTERS

The Great White shark has been called a "man-eater," but other species are just as deadly. Some sharks will hunt anything they can bite and swallow. With a combination of speed, bulk, and a huge appetite they hunt with great concentration.

Lemon shark

The Lemon shark prefers shallow water where it hunts for fish, rays, and crustaceans. It has a yellow-brown colored body and sharp, narrow teeth.

HUNTING COLORS

Sharks that swim near the surface are dark on top and lighter underneath. When hunting, this makes them difficult to see from above and below.

Dusky shark

This slow-moving shark has triangular-shaped upper teeth. It hunts for fish, eels, and other sharks, but is not a fussy eater and will grab anything in its path.

The Silky shark is a quick swimmer.

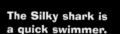

Silky shark

The smooth appearance of its skin gives this shark its name. This dangerous shark has been known to act aggressively toward divers by arching its back and raising its head, as if preparing to attack!

Galapagos shark

The Galapagos shark usually swims in schools and is often found near the seabed where it hunts for fish. It has been known to act in a hostile manner toward human divers.

The Bronze whaler probably owes its name to its coloring, though it can also be gray.

Bronze Whaler

This shark hunts and chases its prey and feeds on other sharks and rays. It has been known to attack swimmers and surfers in shallow water.

The Galapagos shark is named after the Galapagos Islands, west of South America, where it was first discovered.

Bull shark (right)

This aggressive shark is the only one able to live in freshwater, where it may come into contact with humans.

The Bull shark is one of the most dangerous sharks in the world.

BIZARRE SHARKS

Living in the deeper, darker parts of the oceans are a number of sharks with unusual or weird features. They barely resemble the torpedo-shaped species and have bodies that look more like eels. Because deeper water is colder, these bizarre sharks have evolved more slowly and so they still retain some of the features of sharks that lived millions of years ago.

Catshark

This shark's cat-like eyes give it its name. It usually stays still during the day and hunts for prey at night.

Frilled shark

The Frilled shark has an eel-like body and holds onto prey with its sharp teeth. It is rarely seen as it spends most of its time thousands of feet down in the ocean.

DID YOU KNOW?

Cookiecutter sharks are slow swimmers and cannot chase prey very well. Instead, they have light organs on their bodies that glow. It is thought that these attract large prey to come close enough to be bitten.

Most Catsharks have a spotted or striped pattern.

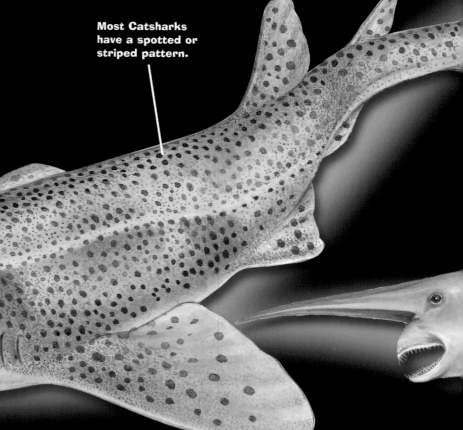

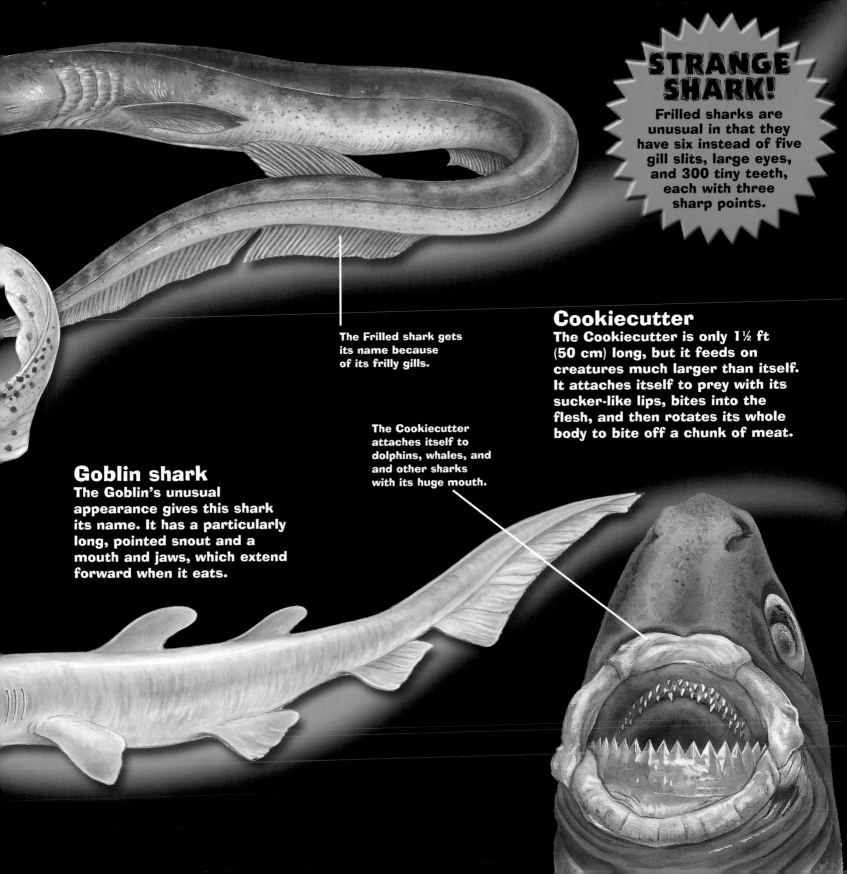

The Frilled shark gets its name because of its frilly gills.

Cookiecutter

The Cookiecutter is only 1½ ft (50 cm) long, but it feeds on creatures much larger than itself. It attaches itself to prey with its sucker-like lips, bites into the flesh, and then rotates its whole body to bite off a chunk of meat.

The Cookiecutter attaches itself to dolphins, whales, and and other sharks with its huge mouth.

Goblin shark

The Goblin's unusual appearance gives this shark its name. It has a particularly long, pointed snout and a mouth and jaws, which extend forward when it eats.

GAPING MOUTHS

Although their sheer size is menacing, the largest sharks are the most harmless. These "gentle giants" swim with their huge mouths wide open to scoop up water. As this passes over their gills, plankton is strained in filters attached to the gills. Some sharks live on the seabed and their wide mouths are armed with sharp-toothed jaws, which grab anything that comes near.

Horn shark
The Horn shark hunts at night for sea urchins and crabs and sucks them into its mouth, crushing them with its strong, rear teeth.

The Whale shark can swim great distances and depths.

HIDING HUNTERS!
Angelsharks and Wobbegongs are masters of camouflage. They have eyes on the tops of their heads to help them see while they lie partially buried on the seabed.

The Whale shark has large pectoral fins and two dorsal fins on its back.

The Angelshark has a flatter body than other sharks and looks similar to rays.

Angelshark
This shark's angel-like shape gives it its name. It lives on the seabed and buries itself in the sand where it waits for fish or squid to swim by. The shark then opens its mouth wide to grab the prey.

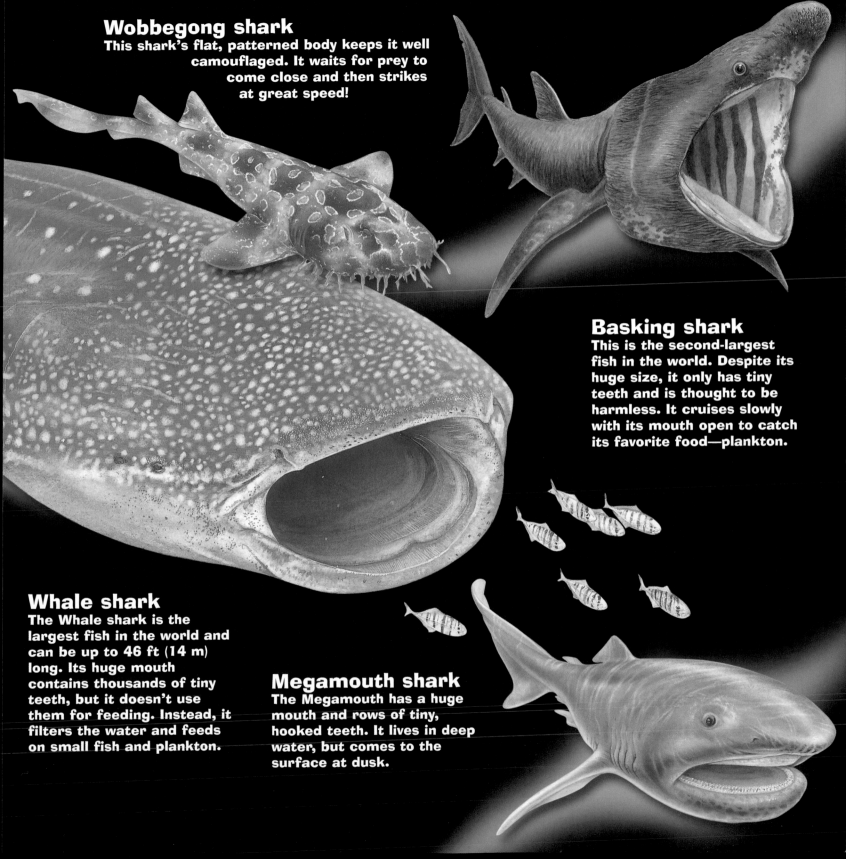

Wobbegong shark
This shark's flat, patterned body keeps it well camouflaged. It waits for prey to come close and then strikes at great speed!

Basking shark
This is the second-largest fish in the world. Despite its huge size, it only has tiny teeth and is thought to be harmless. It cruises slowly with its mouth open to catch its favorite food—plankton.

Whale shark
The Whale shark is the largest fish in the world and can be up to 46 ft (14 m) long. Its huge mouth contains thousands of tiny teeth, but it doesn't use them for feeding. Instead, it filters the water and feeds on small fish and plankton.

Megamouth shark
The Megamouth has a huge mouth and rows of tiny, hooked teeth. It lives in deep water, but comes to the surface at dusk.

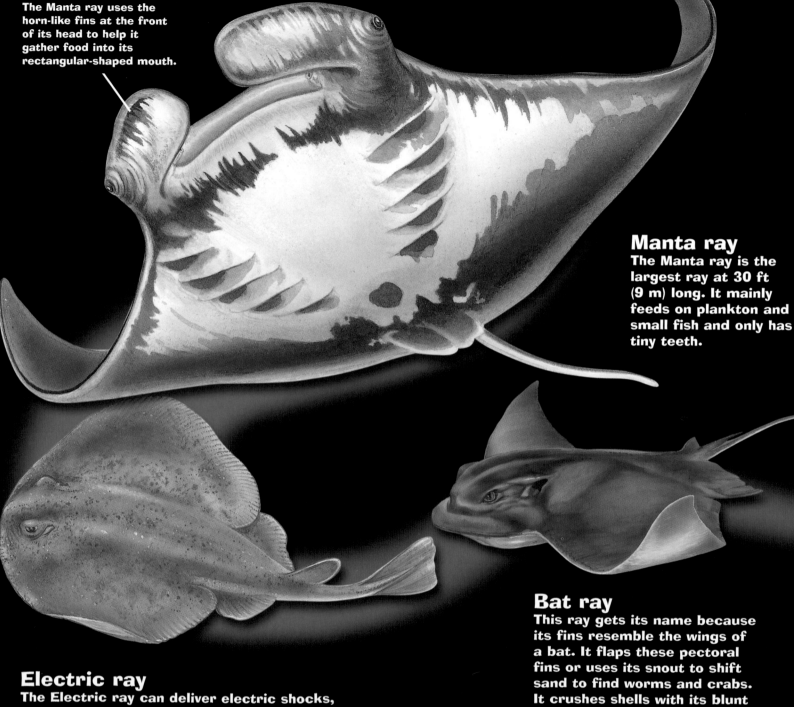

The Manta ray uses the horn-like fins at the front of its head to help it gather food into its rectangular-shaped mouth.

Manta ray

The Manta ray is the largest ray at 30 ft (9 m) long. It mainly feeds on plankton and small fish and only has tiny teeth.

Electric ray

The Electric ray can deliver electric shocks, which can stun prey and humans and keep predators away. It usually rests during the day and hunts for fish at night, which it usually swallows whole.

Bat ray

This ray gets its name because its fins resemble the wings of a bat. It flaps these pectoral fins or uses its snout to shift sand to find worms and crabs. It crushes shells with its blunt teeth and has a stinging spine that it uses to deliver venom into its enemies.

REMARKABLE RAYS

JUMPING RAY!
Manta rays have huge pectoral fins up to 23 ft (7 m) across. They can leap up to 5 ft (1.5 m) out of the water and can do somersaults.

Eagle ray
This ray uses its large fins to swim gracefully and can leap above the water to escape predators. It also has a venomous spine.

Stingray
The Stingray has a razor-sharp spine, which can deliver a painful sting.

Torpedo ray
The Torpedo ray is an excellent predator and can deliver an electric shock of more than 200 volts, which is strong enough to stun a human.

Rays share many features with their cousins the sharks, but the main difference between them is body shape. Instead of a streamlined, torpedo-shape, rays have a flattened body with the pectoral fins joined to the head. Also, their gill slits, nostrils, and mouths are on their undersides. Some use large pectoral fins like wings to move gracefully, while others use their tails for thrust.

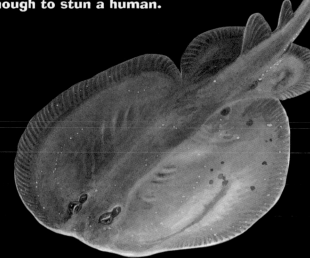

The Leopard seal has a spotted coat and uses powerful jaws and sharp teeth to catch prey.

Leopard seal

This seal lives in the Antarctic, so doesn't compete with sharks, but is the deadliest seal predator.

Moray eel

This eel uses its sense of smell to find prey, which it kills with its long teeth.

FIERCE RIVALS

Sharks are not the only predators in the oceans. A variety of other fierce animals compete with them for food. Some sharks (especially young ones and smaller species) even make a tasty meal! Rivals tend to hide away and use an ambush technique to catch prey. Others are fast-moving predators. All these competitors have large, tooth-filled jaws that can quickly tear prey to shreds.

Killer whale

The Killer whale is an incredibly fast swimmer. It hunts in family pods and feeds on seals, sea lions, and other whales. It has even been known to grab seals from land.

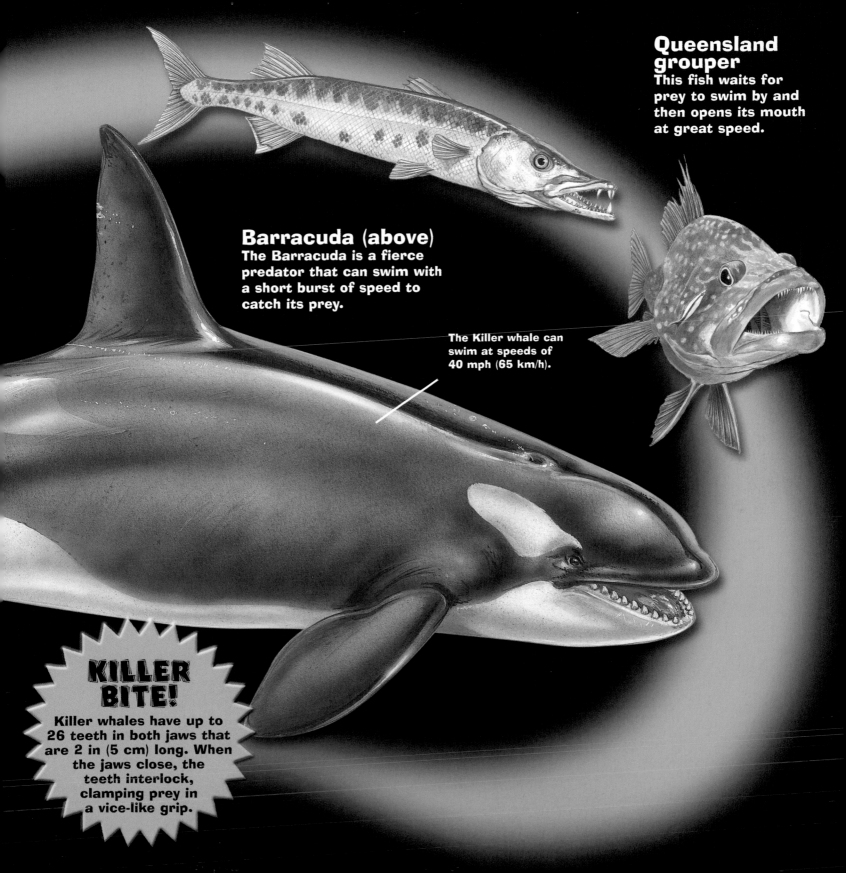

Queensland grouper
This fish waits for prey to swim by and then opens its mouth at great speed.

Barracuda (above)
The Barracuda is a fierce predator that can swim with a short burst of speed to catch its prey.

The Killer whale can swim at speeds of 40 mph (65 km/h).

KILLER BITE!
Killer whales have up to 26 teeth in both jaws that are 2 in (5 cm) long. When the jaws close, the teeth interlock, clamping prey in a vice-like grip.

OCEAN GIANTS

Sharks share the oceans with other huge creatures including whales. Although whales have a fish-shaped, hairless body and flipper-like front limbs, they are actually mammals. Instead of using gills for breathing, they need to rise to the water's surface and use lungs to breathe air. They have reasonable vision, but have extraordinarily sensitive hearing.

Blue whale
The Blue whale can be 110 ft (33.5 m) long and is the largest animal to have ever lived on Earth. Even newborn calves can be 25 ft (7.5 m) long! Despite its huge size, the Blue whale prefers small prey and feeds on krill.

Sei whale
This whale can be 50 ft (15 m) long and is one of the fastest whales. It can reach speeds of 30 mph (48 km/h).

The Sperm whale can dive deeper than any other mammal.

Sperm whale
The Sperm whale has the heaviest brain of any living creature, and has a huge head that can be about a third of its body length.

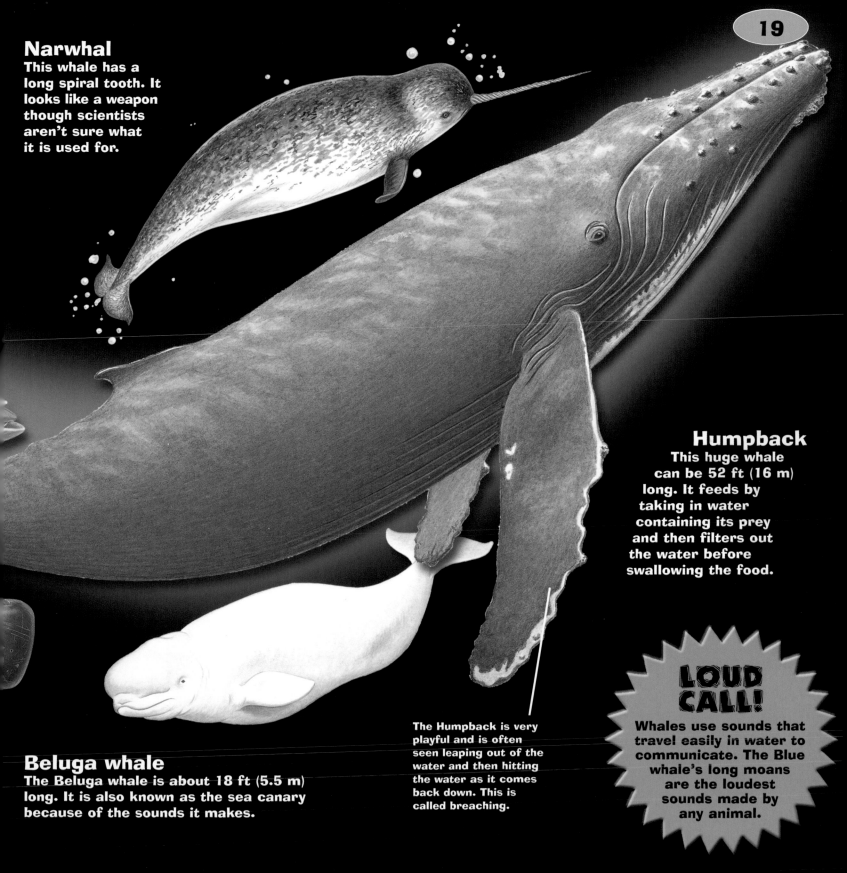

Narwhal
This whale has a long spiral tooth. It looks like a weapon though scientists aren't sure what it is used for.

Humpback
This huge whale can be 52 ft (16 m) long. It feeds by taking in water containing its prey and then filters out the water before swallowing the food.

The Humpback is very playful and is often seen leaping out of the water and then hitting the water as it comes back down. This is called breaching.

Beluga whale
The Beluga whale is about 18 ft (5.5 m) long. It is also known as the sea canary because of the sounds it makes.

LOUD CALL!
Whales use sounds that travel easily in water to communicate. The Blue whale's long moans are the loudest sounds made by any animal.

The Sawfish's long snout has a series of sharp teeth on either side.

SAWS AND SWORDS

Some shark-shaped fish have long snouts. Those with saw-like snouts probe and scavenge for food on the seabed. Fish with "swords" hunt in open water and, with their streamlined shape, are capable of reaching speeds of at least 50 mph (80 km/h). These species use their "swords" to stun or thrash prey to death before it is eaten.

SHARP BLADE

The Sawfish, which looks like a cross between a shark and a ray, has a flattened blade, which is more than 39 in (1 m) long and is edged with at least 50 sharp teeth.

Blue marlin (left)

The Blue marlin attacks schools of fish, such as tuna, at high speed. It uses its sharp, pointed snout to stun and kill.

Sawfish (left)

The Sawfish is one of the largest fish in the ocean. Its long snout has a series of sharp teeth on either side. It feeds on small fish and invertebrates and will attack fish with its snout before eating them.

Swordfish (below)

The Swordfish has a flattened snout with sharp edges. It is an aggressive hunter and uses its "sword" to stun or thrash prey to death.

DID YOU KNOW?

The Elephant fish's snout is equipped with a type of electrical sensor. This means that the snout acts like a scanning device and detects prey hidden in the seabed. The fish then uses the snout to dig the prey out.

Elephant fish

The Elephant fish is so-named because of its unusual trunk-like snout. It usually swims at depths of 650 ft (200 m) and uses its snout to search for prey on the seabed. It then uses its crushing jaws to eat its catch.

Sawshark

The Sawshark has a long, thin snout with sharp teeth on either side. It uses its snout to probe the seabed for food. It also has long sense organs called barbels on either side of its head, which help it to detect prey.

The Swordfish is an aggressive predator.

TENTACLES AND SUCKERS

Cephalopods are creatures that catch their food and ward off predators using sucker-bearing tentacles. The word cephalopod means "head-footed ones" because they have a head surrounded by tentacles. They also have a beak-like jaw to bite prey and move through the water by means of jet propulsion. Suckers are used to hold on to prey while it is carried to the mouth.

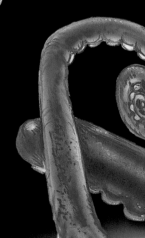

Giant squid
The Giant squid is the largest invertebrate in the world. It has eight tentacles with rows of deadly suckers and two longer tentacles to capture prey before crushing the creature in its powerful jaws.

Blue-ringed octopus
This octopus kills prey with a bite. Its venom is so powerful that it can kill a human in minutes. Its blue markings tell predators to stay away.

The Blue-ringed octopus grabs its prey with its tentacles.

Giant cuttlefish
The Giant cuttlefish has 10 tentacles around its mouth. Two are longer than the others and have hooks for catching prey.

Nautilus
The Nautilus swims slowly or crawls at the bottom of the ocean. It uses the tentacles around its mouth to grab fish and crabs.

SHARP SENSES!

The eyes of an octopus, like those of a shark, can adapt to rapid changes in the amount of light in the water as it moves from the ocean depths to the surface.

Giant Pacific octopus

This is the largest octopus. It holds prey with its tentacles and eats the animal with its beak-like mouth. It can be aggressive and has been known to attack sharks and birds.

The Vampire squid's tentacles have a series of jagged spines along their edges.

Vampire squid

The Vampire squid isn't a true squid. It has eight tentacles that are joined together by a web of skin.

Like other octopuses, the Giant Pacific has eight long tentacles.

CLAWS AND PINCERS

Crustaceans share the oceans with sharks. They have small mouths and so use claws and pincers to catch prey. They also use them to fight off attackers. The crustacean shape varies, but they have several common features. They have two pairs of antennae, eyes on stalks, a tough, outer covering/shell, and several pairs of legs, the first pair of which may form large powerful claws or pincers.

Emperor shrimp
This shrimp uses its pincers to feed on parasites on the Sea Cucumber's body.

Japanese Spider
This crab can live to be 100 years old. It is the largest crustacean and can weigh as much as 44 lb (20 kg).

The Japanese Spider crab can grow to be 12 ft (3.7 m) wide.

The Harlequin shrimp is one of the most colorful creatures in the ocean.

CRAB LEGS!

Due to its strange shape, the Japanese Spider crab can only move about in very still waters. On land, it is completely helpless and cannot even raise itself upright.

Harlequin shrimp

This shrimp works in pairs to attack its favorite food, starfish. It uses its paddle-like front pincers to pull the starfish off of a rock and then turns it over before feeding on the feet.

DID YOU KNOW?

Horseshoe crabs are living fossils. They have existed and remained virtually unchanged for more than 200 million years. The horseshoe's five pairs of legs push the armor-plated creature through mud.

Ghost crab

This crab covers itself in sand, so only its eyes on stalks can be seen. This means it often seems to appear and disappear when it moves.

North Atlantic lobster

This lobster is one of the heaviest crustaceans. It has huge front pincers that it uses to hold on to its prey. Like other crustaceans, it can regrow damaged claws or antennae.

Horseshoe crab

The Horseshoe crab isn't really a crab, but is an invertebrate with a hard outer shell. It has five pairs of legs with pincers and a sharp tail, which it uses to change direction.

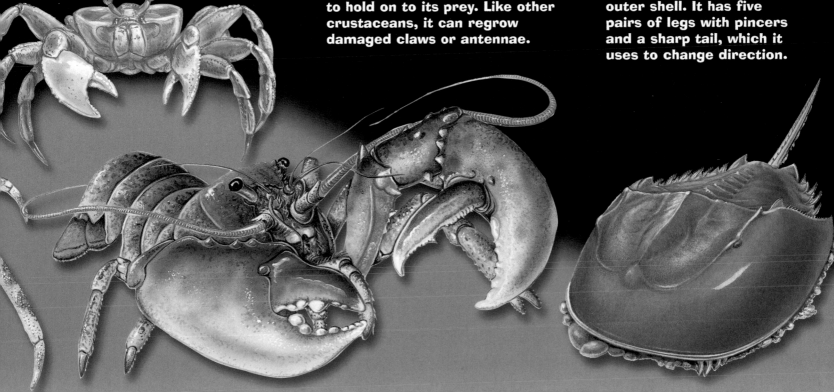

DON'T TOUCH!

Looks can be deceptive! Some of the most seemingly harmless sea creatures are the most dangerous. Unlike most sharks that actively hunt prey, these are either slow movers or are still. Beneath an attractive exterior they hide powerful weapons loaded with stinging cells to stun or kill their prey. This poison is often their only means of defense. Their bright colors warn others of the dangers.

Lionfish
The Lionfish is one of the most dangerous fish in the ocean. Its striking color and appearance warn predators to stay away. The Lionfish usually feeds at night and will use its fins to trap its prey before eating it.

The Lionfish's dorsal fin contains several spines filled with venom.

Sea urchin
The urchin's body and shell is covered in sharp spines. They protect it from prey and can cause a nasty wound.

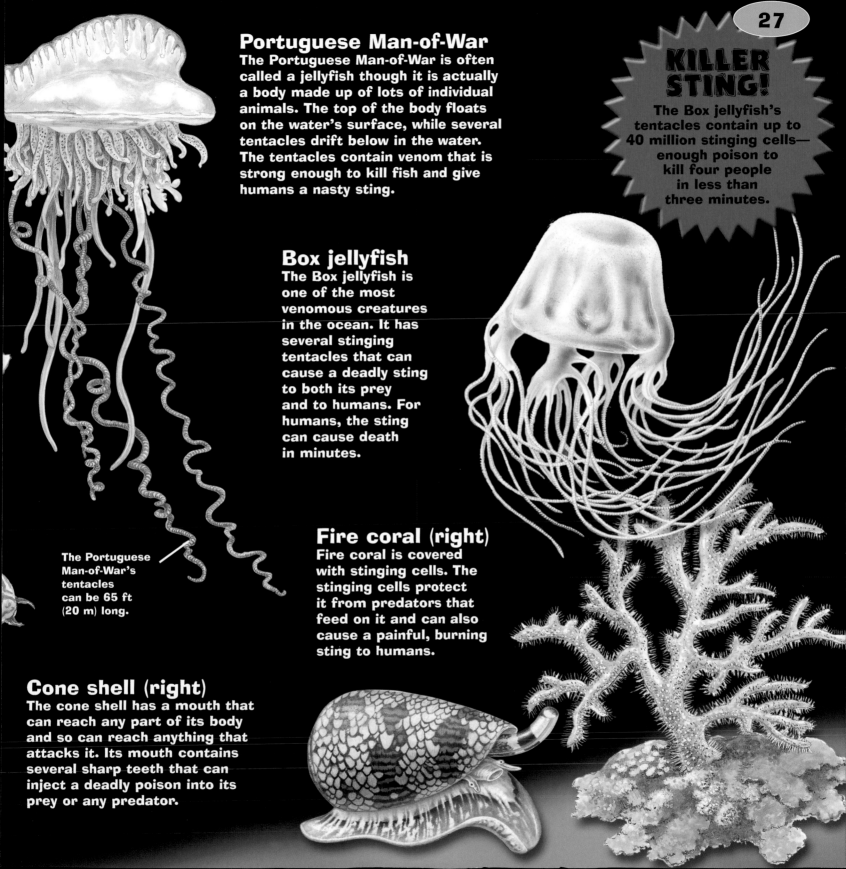

Portuguese Man-of-War

The Portuguese Man-of-War is often
called a jellyfish though it is actually
a body made up of lots of individual
animals. The top of the body floats
on the water's surface, while several
tentacles drift below in the water.
The tentacles contain venom that is
strong enough to kill fish and give
humans a nasty sting.

KILLER STING!

The Box jellyfish's
tentacles contain up to
40 million stinging cells—
enough poison to
kill four people
in less than
three minutes.

Box jellyfish

The Box jellyfish is
one of the most
venomous creatures
in the ocean. It has
several stinging
tentacles that can
cause a deadly sting
to both its prey
and to humans. For
humans, the sting
can cause death
in minutes.

The Portuguese
Man-of-War's
tentacles
can be 65 ft
(20 m) long.

Fire coral (right)

Fire coral is covered
with stinging cells. The
stinging cells protect
it from predators that
feed on it and can also
cause a painful, burning
sting to humans.

Cone shell (right)

The cone shell has a mouth that
can reach any part of its body
and so can reach anything that
attacks it. Its mouth contains
several sharp teeth that can
inject a deadly poison into its
prey or any predator.

The Viperfish swallows prey whole. Its stomach expands, so it can eat prey almost as large as itself.

Viperfish

The Viperfish has long, needle-sharp teeth, which are too big to fit inside its mouth. It opens its mouth wide and pierces prey with its sharp fangs.

Dragonfish

The Dragonfish has a long, slim body and curved, needle-like teeth. It has light organs along its body and on its barbel, which dangles from its chin, to attract prey close to its jaws.

TERRORS OF THE DEEP

Mysterious and unfamiliar fish live in the icy cold, dark waters of the ocean depths. They survive in these harsh conditions using a variety of techniques. Many would die if they found themselves in shallower, warmer seas. About 90 percent of the creatures living in the depths can produce their own light. They use this light to communicate, to attract food, and for camouflage. Many of these creatures have a large head to grab prey.

Bristlemouth

This fish is usually found in deep water, but rises to the surface to feed. While near the surface, it can send out two rows of light from the underside of its body. This light camouflages it from any predators below.

The Bristlemouth has long, sharp bristle-like teeth.

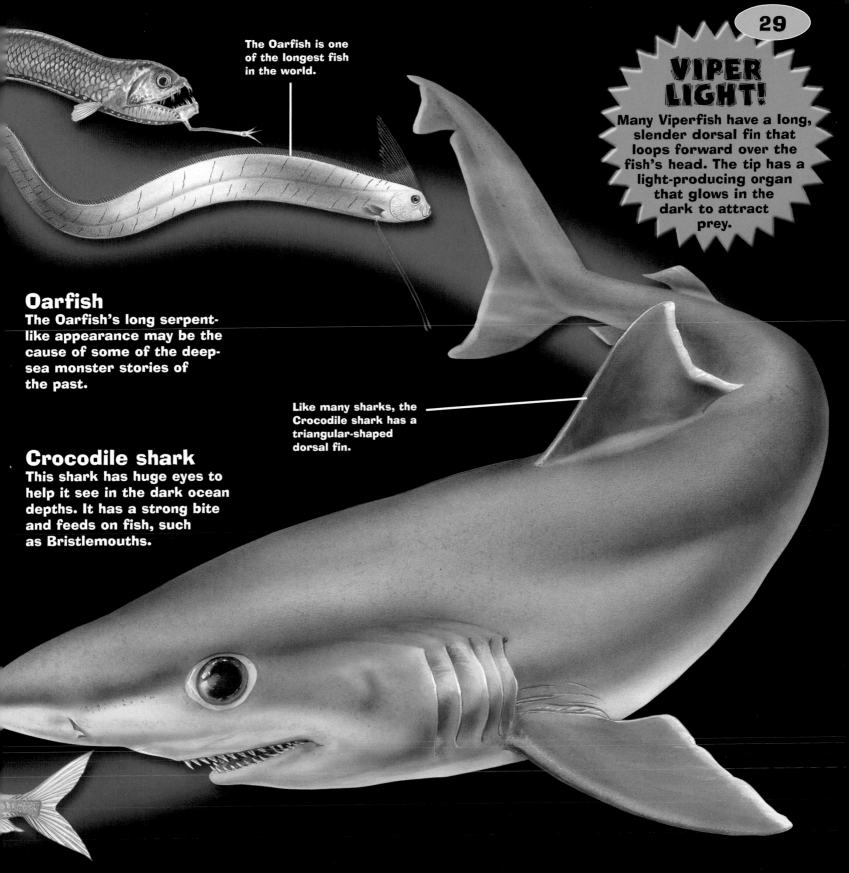

The Oarfish is one of the longest fish in the world.

VIPER LIGHT!

Many Viperfish have a long, slender dorsal fin that loops forward over the fish's head. The tip has a light-producing organ that glows in the dark to attract prey.

Oarfish

The Oarfish's long serpent-like appearance may be the cause of some of the deep-sea monster stories of the past.

Like many sharks, the Crocodile shark has a triangular-shaped dorsal fin.

Crocodile shark

This shark has huge eyes to help it see in the dark ocean depths. It has a strong bite and feeds on fish, such as Bristlemouths.

GLOSSARY

Antenna
A thin sense organ on the top of the head of an insect or crustacean, used to feel, hear, and smell. There are always two antennae.

Barbel
A thin sense organ around the mouths or under the chin of certain fish. It is often used to detect prey.

Cartilage
An elastic-like tissue that makes up part of the skeleton.

Cephalopod
An animal with tentacles around its head. Squid and octopuses are cephalopods.

Crustacean
An animal with a hard outer shell and jointed legs, which is usually found in the ocean. Crabs, shrimp, and lobsters are crustaceans.

Fin
A body part on the back, sides, or underside of a fish, used for swimming and guiding the body. The dorsal fin refers to the fin on the back. The pectoral fins are the fins toward the front of the sides of the fish.

Gill
An organ used for breathing in water on the heads of fish and some other animals. There are usually one or more gill slits on the sides of the head.

Invertebrate
An animal that does not have a backbone. Insects, octopuses, and squid are invertebrates.

Krill
Small, shrimp-like animals found in the ocean, which are an important food for many animals.

Plankton
Tiny animals and plants that float in the water.

Pod
A small group of marine animals, such as dolphins, whales, or seals.

Predator
An animal that hunts and eats other animals.

Prey
An animal that is hunted and eaten by other animals.

School
A large group of fish.

Spine
A sharp part of the body on fish that is often poisonous.

Venom
A poison produced by an animal and released by biting or stinging.

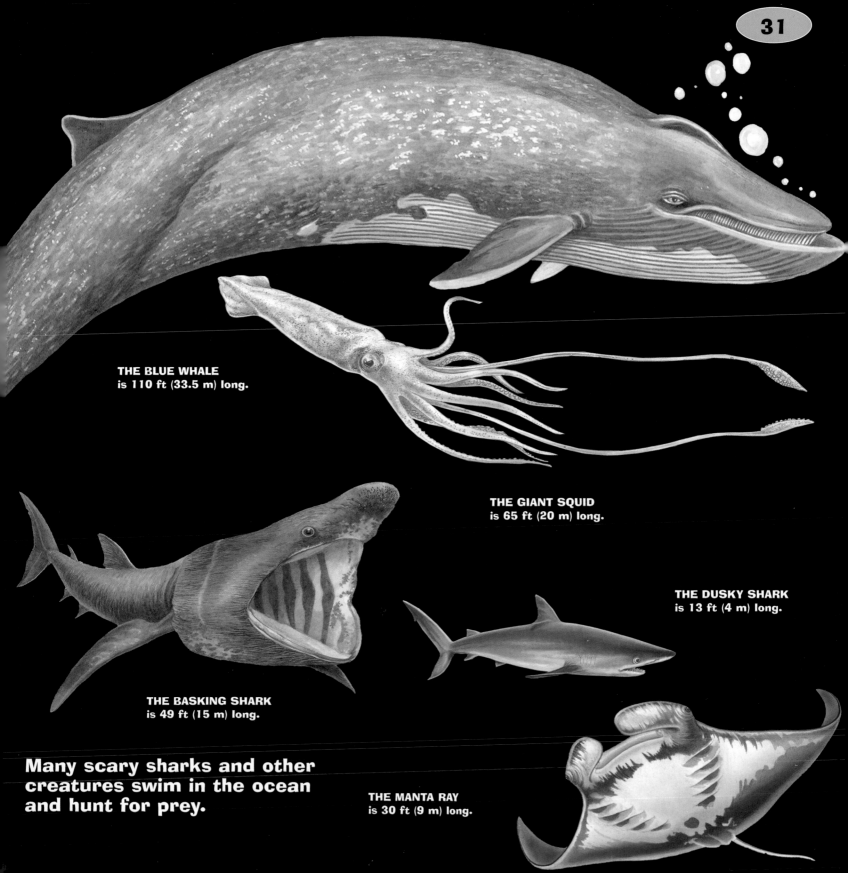

THE BLUE WHALE
is 110 ft (33.5 m) long.

THE GIANT SQUID
is 65 ft (20 m) long.

THE DUSKY SHARK
is 13 ft (4 m) long.

THE BASKING SHARK
is 49 ft (15 m) long.

Many scary sharks and other
creatures swim in the ocean
and hunt for prey.

THE MANTA RAY
is 30 ft (9 m) long.

INDEX

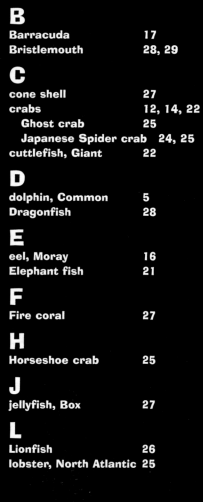